LE CORDON BLEU

HOME COLLECTION
·SEAFOOD·

MEREHURST

contents

recipe ratings ❁ *easy* ❁❁ *a little more care needed* ❁❁❁ *more care needed*

Lobster bisque

Smooth, creamy bisques are thought to have Spanish origins, where in the province of Biscay they may originally have been made with pigeons or quail until shellfish took over as the main ingredient in the seventeenth century.

*Preparation time **30 minutes***
*Total cooking time **30 minutes***
Serves 4

1 large or 2 small uncooked lobsters,
about 700–800 g (1 lb 7 oz–1 lb 10 oz) in total
2 tablespoons olive oil
$1/2$ carrot, cut into cubes
$1/2$ onion, cut into cubes
$1/2$ small celery stick, cut into cubes
$2^{1}/2$ tablespoons brandy
150 ml (5 fl oz) dry white wine
4 large tomatoes, peeled, seeded and quartered
or 50 g ($1^{3}/4$ oz) passata
1 bouquet garni (see Chef's tip)
1.5 litres fish stock
85 g ($2^{3}/4$ oz) rice flour
2 egg yolks
1 tablespoon thick (double) cream
1 teaspoon finely chopped fresh tarragon

1 If you have bought live lobsters, kill them according to the method in the Chef's techniques on page 61. If you prefer not to do this, ask your fishmonger to do it.
2 Prepare the lobster following the method in the Chef's techniques on page 61. Heat the oil in a large pan, add the lobster pieces in their shell and stir for 2 minutes over high heat. Add the carrot, onion and celery, reduce the heat and cook for 2 minutes. Add the brandy and immediately ignite at arm's length, then allow the flames to subside or cover with a lid. Pour in the wine and stir to blend in any sticky juices from the pan base. Add the tomato or passata, bouquet garni and stock and bring to the boil.
3 Using a slotted spoon, remove the lobster pieces from the stock, roughly break into small pieces using a knife and return to the pan with the rice flour. Stir to combine, bring to the boil and simmer for 10 minutes.
4 Pass the soup through a fine sieve, pressing the solids with the back of a spoon to extract all the juices, then discard the contents of the sieve, pour the liquid into a clean pan and season with salt and black pepper. The bisque should just coat the back of a spoon. If not, bring to the boil and simmer to reduce.
5 In a bowl, mix the egg yolks and cream together, stir in about 125 ml (4 fl oz) of the hot bisque, then pour back into the bisque. Check the seasoning and reheat for 5 minutes, stirring continuously, without boiling. Sprinkle over the tarragon and serve in warm bowls or a soup tureen.

Chef's tip To make the bouquet garni, wrap the green part of a leek loosely around a bay leaf, a sprig of thyme, some celery leaves and a few stalks of parsley, then tie with string. Leave a long tail to the string for easy removal.

Ceviche

Ceviche originated in South America and is the perfect way to show off the freshest fish. The acidity of the lime dressing magically 'cooks' the raw fish until it is opaque, just as if heat had been used.

Preparation time 55 minutes + 4 hours refrigeration
Total cooking time 1 minute
Serves 6

600 g (1 1/4 lb) bream, snapper or seabass fillets,
  skinned (see Chef's tips)
juice of 6 limes
1 small onion, finely chopped
1 green capsicum (pepper), halved, seeded and
  finely chopped
1/2 red chilli, seeded and finely chopped
1/2 cucumber, cut into 5 mm (1/4 inch) cubes
1 small avocado, peeled and cut into 5 mm
  (1/4 inch) cubes
4 tomatoes, peeled, seeded and diced
few sprigs of fresh parsley or chervil, to garnish

WATERCRESS VINAIGRETTE
100 g (3 1/4 oz) watercress, tough stems removed
1 1/4 tablespoons white wine vinegar
100 ml (3 1/4 fl oz) olive oil

1 Cut the bream, snapper or seabass fillets into 5 mm
(1/4 inch) wide slices, pour over the lime juice, cover
and refrigerate for about 2 hours.

2 Drain the fish, then add some salt and black pepper,
the onion, capsicum, chilli, cucumber and avocado and
mix gently to combine. Cover with plastic wrap and
refrigerate for 1–2 hours. Chill six serving plates.

3 To make the watercress vinaigrette, add the
watercress to a pan of boiling salted water and cook for
about 1 minute, then drain and run under cold water.
Pat dry with paper towels to remove excess water, then
purée in a blender or food processor with the white
wine vinegar and olive oil. Season with some salt and
black pepper.

4 To serve, place an 8 cm (3 inch) pastry cutter in the
centre of a chilled plate and spoon the ceviche into it
until full, packing down lightly with the back of a
spoon. Remove the cutter and repeat on the other
plates. Decorate the plates with the watercress
vinaigrette and garnish with the diced tomato and
parsley or chervil. Serve with some crusty bread.

Chef's tips If you can only buy a whole bream, snapper
or seabass, buy an 800 g (1 lb 10 oz) fish and fillet it
yourself (see Chef's techniques, page 63).

For a more creamy variation to this dish, add 250 ml
(8 fl oz) coconut milk with the vegetables.

Gravlax

A Scandinavian method of curing salmon in salt, sugar and dill. The salmon is left to marinate for 1½ days and is then served with a traditional sweet dill and mustard dressing.

*Preparation time **1 hour + 36 hours refrigeration***
*Total cooking time **Nil***
Serves 10

1.8 kg (3 lb 10 oz) salmon fillet, skin on
  but scales removed
115 g (3³/4 oz) rock or sea salt
85 g (2³/4 oz) caster sugar
4 tablespoons chopped fresh dill
1¹/2 tablespoons black peppercorns, crushed
2 teaspoons coriander seeds, crushed
1 teaspoon ground mixed spice
6 tablespoons roughly chopped fresh dill leaves

DILL AND MUSTARD DRESSING
2 teaspoons sweet mustard (German) or 2 teaspoons
  grain mustard mixed with 2 teaspoons honey
2 teaspoons chopped fresh dill
2 teaspoons white wine vinegar or cider vinegar
220 ml (7 fl oz) vegetable oil

1 Wash the salmon, dry it with paper towels and lay on a tray or plate, skin-side-down. Mix together the salt, sugar, dill, peppercorns, coriander seeds and mixed spice and spoon it over the fish. Cover with plastic wrap, place a baking tray on top and a roughly 500 g (1 lb) weight to lightly press the salmon (this could be cans spaced out along the fish). Refrigerate for 24 hours.

2 Remove the weights and covering, discard the solids from the marinade, then rinse the remaining marinade off with cold water and pat the salmon dry with paper towels. Place on a clean tray or plate, skin-side-down.

3 Press the dill leaves onto the salmon, then cover with plastic wrap and press well with your fingers to make the dill adhere. Refrigerate for 12 hours.

4 To make the dill and mustard dressing, mix all the ingredients except the oil together in a bowl with some salt and black pepper, then slowly drizzle the oil into the bowl, whisking to emulsify with the other ingredients.

5 Uncover the salmon, remove any excess dill, then lift onto a board. With a long, thin-bladed knife held at an angle of 45 degrees and about 6–8 cm (2¹/2–3 inches) from the tail, cut a slice towards the tail and continue slicing to produce short thin slices. Serve with the dressing.

Chef's tip For a variation, try this beetroot and mustard mixture. Follow the recipe to the end of Step 2, then combine 50 g (1³/4 oz) mustard seeds (soaked in cold water for 30 minutes, then drained) and 250 g (8 oz) very finely chopped cooked beetroot. Press onto the salmon and continue as above.

Gravlax (top) and Beetroot and mustard gravlax

Seafood paella

A classic Spanish dish consisting of rice and saffron, often combined with chicken, pork and chorizo, although here we use seafood only. The name is derived from the large two-handled dish in which the paella is traditionally cooked and served.

Preparation time **45 minutes**
Total cooking time **45 minutes**
Serves 4

3 pinches of saffron threads
3 tablespoons olive oil
1 large onion, sliced
300 g (10 oz) long-grain rice
3 tomatoes, peeled, seeded and roughly chopped or
  400 g (12 3/4 oz) can chopped tomatoes, drained
2 cloves garlic, crushed
550 ml (18 fl oz) chicken or vegetable stock
300 g (10 oz) mussels, scrubbed and beards removed
  (see page 62)
16 large raw prawns, shells on
1 cooked crab in its shell, cleaned and cut
  into quarters, or 4 cooked crab claws
  in their shells (see Chef's tips)
300 g (10 oz) small clams, cockles or pipi, well washed
150 g (5 oz) firm white fish fillets, skinned and
  cut into 3 cm (1 1/4 inch) pieces
90 g (3 oz) frozen baby peas
1 red capsicum (pepper), cut into 2.5 cm (1 inch)
  lengths and thinly sliced

1 Place the saffron threads in a small bowl and soak in 2 tablespoons hot water.

2 Heat the oil in a paellera or heavy-based frying pan, 30–35 cm (12–14 inches) in diameter, add the onion and cook for about 3–4 minutes, or until soft. Add the rice and saffron and cook, stirring, for 2 minutes. Add the tomato, garlic and stock and bring to the boil. Reduce the heat and stir in half the mussels, prawns, crab, clams and fish with all the peas and red capsicum. Season well with salt and black pepper.

3 Arrange the remaining seafood on top and cover with a piece of greaseproof paper and a lid. Cook over low heat for 30 minutes, or until the rice is tender and the liquid has been absorbed. Don't stir the paella while it cooks as this will break up the fish and make the finished dish look messy. If the liquid has been absorbed but the rice is not cooked, add a little extra water and continue cooking until the rice is cooked through. Discard any unopened mussels and serve immediately.

Chef's tips Paella is traditionally served directly from the paellera or pan. If you are using a frying pan, check it is deep enough (3–5 cm/1 1/4–2 inches) to hold the liquid.

To clean a crab, remove the stomach sac and grey spongy fingers (gills).

Coquilles Saint-Jacques mornay

Coquilles Saint Jacques is the French term for scallops, meaning Saint James's shells. Here they are baked in the half shell and classically coated beneath piped potato and a Gruyère cheese sauce.

Preparation time **25 minutes**
Total cooking time **45 minutes**
Serves 4

8 large fresh scallops in their shells
55 g (1 3/4 oz) Gruyère cheese, finely grated

DUCHESSE POTATOES
1 kg (2 lb) floury potatoes, peeled and cut
 into pieces
25 g (3/4 oz) unsalted butter
2 egg yolks
pinch of grated nutmeg

MORNAY SAUCE
15 g (1/2 oz) unsalted butter
15 g (1/2 oz) plain flour
250 ml (8 fl oz) milk
1 egg yolk
55 g (1 3/4 oz) Gruyère cheese, grated

1 To prepare the scallops, follow the method in the Chef's techniques on page 62. Place the scallops flat on a board and slice each one into three circles, leaving the orange roe whole. Cover and refrigerate until needed.
2 Scrub the scallop shells and place in a pan of cold water, bring to the boil and simmer for 5 minutes. Drain and leave the shells to cool and dry.
3 To make the duchesse potatoes, place the potatoes in a large pan of salted, cold water. Cover and bring to the boil, then reduce the heat and simmer for 15–20 minutes, or until the potatoes are tender to the point of a sharp knife. Drain, return to the pan and shake over low heat for 1–2 minutes to remove excess moisture. Mash or push through a fine sieve into a bowl, then stir in the butter and egg yolks and season with nutmeg, salt and black pepper. Spoon the mixture into a piping bag with a 1.5 cm (5/8 inch) star nozzle. Preheat the oven to moderately hot 200°C (400°F/Gas 6).
4 To make the mornay sauce, melt the butter in a heavy-based pan over low-medium heat. Sprinkle over the flour and cook for 1 minute without allowing it to colour, stirring continuously with a wooden spoon. Remove from the heat and slowly add the milk, blending thoroughly. Return to the heat and bring slowly to the boil, stirring constantly. Lower the heat and cook for 3–4 minutes, or until the sauce coats the back of a spoon. Remove from the stove and stir in the egg yolk and cheese, then season with some salt and black pepper.
5 Pipe shell shapes or small overlapping circles of duchesse potato to form a border around the edge of each shell. Place on a baking tray with a rim so that the round edge of each shell rests on the rim to stop the filling running out. Place a sliced scallop and whole roe in each rounded shell, season with salt and black pepper and spoon over the mornay sauce. Sprinkle the cheese over the sauce and bake for about 12–15 minutes, or until golden brown.

Smoked trout pâté

*A stylish but easy-to-make pâté, with a combination of fresh and smoked trout. For a variation,
you could also use smoked and fresh salmon or mackerel.*

*Preparation time **30 minutes + cooling +
1 hour refrigeration***
*Total cooking time **5 minutes***
Serves 6

1 tablespoon white wine vinegar
1 bay leaf
4 white peppercorns
115 g (3³/4 oz) fresh trout fillet, skin on
315 g (10 oz) smoked trout fillet, skinned
200 g (6¹/2 oz) cream cheese
100 g (3¹/4 oz) unsalted butter, softened
3 teaspoons fresh lemon juice
**4 sprigs fresh parsley, chervil or dill,
   to garnish**

1 Place the vinegar, bay leaf, peppercorns and 100 ml
(3¹/4 fl oz) water in a shallow pan and bring slowly to
simmering point. Place the fresh trout skin-side-down in
this poaching liquid, cover and gently cook for about
3–4 minutes, or until cooked through. Allow to cool in
the liquid. Using a fish slice or spatula, lift the trout onto
a plate and remove and discard the skin and any bones.
2 Place the fresh and smoked trout in a food processor
and process to a smooth purée. Add the cream cheese,
butter, lemon juice and some salt and black pepper and
process until all the ingredients are thoroughly
combined. Divide the pâté among six 250 ml (8 fl oz)
ramekins, about 8 cm (3 inches) in diameter, and place
in the refrigerator for 1 hour. To serve, garnish with a
sprig of parsley, chervil or dill and accompany with
Melba toast.

Chef's tip This makes an excellent cocktail dip if served
soft at cool room temperature. Alternatively, pipe it
onto small rounds of toast as a canapé and garnish with
a sprig of dill or chervil.

Sardines with walnut and parsley topping

A crisp walnut topping gives these grilled fresh sardines a lovely texture. They can be served as a main course or appetizer with warm olive oil, lemon wedges, rocket leaves and plenty of fresh bread.

Preparation time **40 minutes**
Total cooking time **20 minutes**
Serves 4

WALNUT AND PARSLEY TOPPING
150 g (5 oz) unsalted butter
4 French shallots, finely chopped
2 cloves garlic, crushed
4 tablespoons fresh white breadcrumbs
110 g (3³/4 oz) walnuts, finely chopped
2 teaspoons finely chopped fresh parsley

16 x 50 g (1³/4 oz) fresh sardines,
 scaled and gutted
2 tablespoons plain flour
50 ml (1³/4 fl oz) olive oil
2 tablespoons olive oil, warm, to serve
lemon wedges, to serve
a few rocket leaves, to serve

1 To make the walnut and parsley topping, melt the butter in a pan over moderate heat, add the shallots and garlic, cover and cook for about 3 minutes, or until soft and translucent. Remove from the stove, season with some salt and black pepper, then add the breadcrumbs, walnuts and parsley and mix thoroughly.

2 Preheat the grill to high. Wash the sardines, then dry well on paper towels. Place the flour on a plate or piece of greaseproof paper and season well with salt and black pepper. Pour the oil onto a separate plate. One at a time, roll the sardines in the flour to coat them, then shake off the excess flour. Dip into the oil, coating on both sides, then transfer half the sardines to the grill pan. Place under the grill and cook for 3 minutes on each side. Remove the first batch to a plate and keep warm while you cook the second batch.

3 Sprinkle the walnut and parsley topping over the sardines and press firmly onto the skin. Return to the grill, in two batches, and cook until the topping is golden brown.

4 Place the sardines on a large serving plate or individual plates and drizzle the warm olive oil around the sardines on the bare areas of the plate. Complete with some black pepper, the lemon wedges and a few rocket leaves.

Coulibiac

A Russian fish pie packed with salmon, rice, hard-boiled eggs and mushrooms, then wrapped in puff pastry to form a pillow shape. A great dish for a party, especially when served with warm beurre blanc.

*Preparation time **50 minutes + 15 minutes refrigeration***
*Total cooking time **1 hour 40 minutes***
*Serves **8***

55 g (1¾ oz) long-grain rice
4 eggs
50 g (1¾ oz) unsalted butter
6 small spring onions, finely sliced
3 large French shallots, finely chopped
400 g (12¾ oz) mushrooms, finely chopped
juice of ½ lemon
500 g (1 lb) salmon fillet, skin on
500 g (1 lb) ready-made puff pastry
2½ tablespoons finely chopped fresh dill
1 egg yolk
100 g (3¼ oz) fromage frais or natural yoghurt

COURT BOUILLON
1 small carrot, roughly chopped
1 small onion, roughly chopped
1 bay leaf
4 fresh parsley stalks
1 sprig fresh thyme
6 black peppercorns
2 tablespoons white wine vinegar

1 Cook the rice until tender, then drain well. Hard-boil 3 of the eggs for 10 minutes, place in a bowl of iced water to cool quickly, then coarsely grate or finely chop.
2 Melt half the butter in a pan and add the spring onion. Cover and cook for 4 minutes over low heat until soft and translucent. Season and set aside.
3 Melt the remaining butter, add the shallots and cook gently for 2 minutes. Add the mushrooms, lemon juice, salt and pepper and cook until the mushrooms are dry.
4 To make the court bouillon, place all the ingredients except the vinegar in a pan with 1.5 litres water and a large pinch of salt. Bring to the boil, then simmer, covered, for 15 minutes. Add the vinegar and simmer for 5 minutes.
5 Add the salmon to the court bouillon and poach, covered, for 5 minutes. Remove from the heat, uncover and let the salmon cool in the liquid before transferring to a plate. Remove the flesh in large flakes from the skin and cover with plastic wrap. Discard any skin and bones.
6 Cut the pastry in half and, on a lightly floured surface, roll out one half to a 3 mm (⅛ inch) thick rectangle. Transfer to a baking tray without a lip and trim down to a rectangle big enough to contain the salmon, about 23 x 35 cm (9 x 14 inches). Wrap and chill the trimmings, layering them flat. Leaving a 2.5 cm (1 inch) border on all sides, spread the rice in the centre of the pastry. Sprinkle over ½ tablespoon of dill, then the salmon, salt and pepper, mushroom mixture, egg and spring onion in separate layers.
7 Beat the remaining egg and brush over the pastry border. Roll the remaining pastry to about 45 x 30 cm (18 x 12 inches), then pick the pastry up on the rolling pin and place over the filling. Press the edges together to seal the top and bottom, then trim neatly and brush with egg. Roll out the reserved trimmings and cut strips to decorate the pie. Lay them on as a lattice and place the pie in the refrigerator for 10–15 minutes.
8 Preheat the oven to moderately hot 200°C (400°F/ Gas 6). Beat the yolk and remaining egg together and brush over the pie. Wipe off any egg from the tray and make three small holes down the centre of the pie with a skewer. Bake for 30 minutes, until risen, crisp and golden.
9 Stir the remaining dill into the fromage frais or yoghurt and serve with slices of the Coulibiac.

Chef's tip For a special dinner, the coulibiac could be served with a beurre blanc sauce (see page 44).

Bouillabaisse

Fishermen in Marseille made this fragrant soup using fish that were difficult to sell. These were tossed into a simmering pot, hence the name Bouillabaisse, from 'bouillir' (to boil) and 'abaisser' (to reduce). You can use any combination of the fish below in the soup, and increase the amount of one fish if another is not available.

Preparation time 1 hour
Total cooking time 1 hour 10 minutes
Serves 4–6

1 John Dory, filleted and bones reserved (see page 63)
2 sole, filleted and bones reserved (see page 63)
500 g (1 lb) monkfish or ling, filleted and
  bones reserved (see page 62)
1 small sea bream, filleted and bones reserved
  (see page 62)
500 g (1 lb) conger eel, cut into pieces
90 ml (3 fl oz) olive oil
2 cloves garlic, finely chopped
pinch of saffron threads
1 carrot, fennel bulb and leek, white part only, cut
  into julienne strips (see Chef's tip)
24 thin slices French baguette, for croûtes
3 cloves garlic, cut in half, for croûtes
chopped fresh basil, to garnish

SOUP
1 small leek, onion and fennel bulb, sliced thinly
1 celery stick, sliced thinly
2 cloves garlic
2 tablespoons tomato paste
500 ml (16 fl oz) white wine
pinch of saffron threads
2 sprigs of fresh thyme
1 bay leaf
4 sprigs of fresh parsley

ROUILLE SAUCE
1 egg yolk
1 tablespoon tomato paste
3 cloves garlic, crushed into a paste

pinch of saffron threads
250 ml (8 fl oz) olive oil
1 baked potato, about 200 g (6 1/2 oz)

1 Season the fish and eel and toss with half the oil, the garlic, saffron, carrot, fennel and leek. Cover and refrigerate.
2 To make the soup, heat the remaining oil in a stockpot over high heat, add the reserved bones and cook for 3 minutes. Stir in the leek, onion, fennel, celery and garlic and cook for 2 minutes, then mix in the tomato paste and cook for 2 minutes. Pour in the wine and simmer for 5 minutes. Finally, add 1 litre water, the saffron and herbs and simmer for 20 minutes. Strain through a sieve, pressing down to extract as much juice as possible, then discard the solids. Place the soup in a pan and simmer for 15 minutes until slightly thickened, skimming to remove any foam that floats to the surface.
3 To make the rouille, whisk the egg yolk in a small bowl with the tomato paste, garlic, saffron and some salt and black pepper. Continue to whisk while slowly pouring the oil into the mixture. Press the flesh of the potato through a sieve and whisk into the sauce.
4 Lightly toast the French baguette under a preheated grill, cool, then rub both sides with the cut sides of the half cloves of garlic to make garlic croûtes. Set aside.
5 Cut each fish fillet into six and add to a large pot with the eel and julienne vegetables. Pour the hot soup over and simmer for 7 minutes, or until the fish is cooked. Remove the fish and vegetables and place in an earthenware or metal dish. Whisk three tablespoons of the rouille into the soup to thicken it a bit, then pour the soup over the fish and sprinkle with the basil. Serve with the garlic croûtes and the remaining rouille.

Chef's tip Julienne strips are strips of vegetables, the size and shape of matchsticks.

Garlic prawns

Ideal as an appetizer or light summer lunch, serve this Spanish-inspired dish with lots of crusty bread to soak up the lemony garlic butter.

Preparation time **20 minutes**
Total cooking time **10 minutes**
Serves 4

120 g (4 oz) endive or frisée
1 red chilli, seeded and very thinly sliced
1 tablespoon fresh chervil leaves
24 medium raw tiger or gamba prawns, shells on
2 teaspoons vegetable or olive oil
4 cloves garlic, crushed
125 g (4 oz) unsalted butter, cut into cubes
finely grated rind and juice of 1 lemon
1 tablespoon finely chopped fresh parsley

1 Mix together the endive or frisée, chilli and chervil leaves and pile onto the centre of four plates.

2 Shell and devein the prawns, removing the heads but leaving the tails intact, following the method in the Chef's techniques on page 60. Place the prawns on a plate and season lightly with salt and black pepper. Heat the oil in a large, heavy-based frying pan. Add the prawns and, over medium-high heat, fry for about 1 minute on each side, or until cooked through. Remove and keep warm.

3 Add the garlic to the pan and cook for 1 minute, then add the cubes of butter and cook for 4 minutes, or until the butter is nut brown. Remove from the stove and add the lemon rind and juice and the parsley.

4 Quickly shake the pan once or twice to combine all the ingredients, then add the prawns and toss briefly to warm through. Immediately arrange the prawns around the salad on the plates with any remaining pan juices poured over the top.

Whole baked salmon with watercress mayonnaise

Baked in foil to retain the salmon's flavour and moist texture, this impressive centrepiece is the perfect dish for a large summer gathering, served with new potatoes and summer vegetables.

Preparation time 1 hour 10 minutes
 + 1 hour refrigeration
Total cooking time 40 minutes
Serves 10–12

1.5–1.75 kg (3–3 1/2 lb) whole fresh salmon, cleaned
   and scaled (ask your fishmonger to gut the fish
   and remove the scales)
1 small onion, thinly sliced
1 small bay leaf
1 sprig fresh thyme
5 fresh parsley stalks
90 ml (3 fl oz) dry white wine
sprigs of watercress, to garnish
lemon wedges, to garnish

WATERCRESS MAYONNAISE
120 g (4 oz) watercress, tough stems removed
315 g (10 oz) whole-egg mayonnaise
few drops of lemon juice

1 Lift up the gill flap behind the cheek of the salmon head and, using kitchen scissors, remove the dark, frilly gills. Repeat on the other side of the fish. If any scales remain, hold the tail and, using the back of a knife, scrape the skin at a slight angle, working towards the head. Trim the fins. Cut across the tail to shorten it by half, then cut a V shape into the tail. Wash the salmon under cold water and open it on the belly side where the fishmonger has slit it. Remove the blood vessel lying along the backbone using a spoon. Rinse and wipe inside and out with paper towels.

2 Preheat the oven to moderate 180°C (350°F/Gas 4). Butter a piece of foil large enough to wrap around the fish and place on a large baking tray. Lay the salmon just off centre and place the onion and herbs inside the belly. Season with salt and black pepper, then pour over the wine. Quickly cover with foil and seal the edges tightly.

3 Bake for 30–40 minutes, or until the fish feels springy and firm to the touch. Open the foil and leave to cool. Remove the flavourings and lift the salmon onto greaseproof paper, draining off any liquid. Prepare the salmon for serving following the Chef's techniques on page 63, then cover with plastic wrap and refrigerate for 1 hour, or until needed.

4 To make the watercress mayonnaise, add the watercress to a pan of boiling salted water and cook for 1 minute, then drain and run under cold water. Pat dry with paper towels to remove excess water, then purée in a blender or food processor. Beat the purée gradually into the mayonnaise. If it is too dry, add a few drops of lemon juice. Season with salt and black pepper.

5 To serve, decorate the fish with some mayonnaise and serve the remainder separately. Garnish with the watercress sprigs and lemon wedges.

American crab cakes

These crispy crab cakes make a perfect light lunch with salad, or you can make lots of small ones to serve as appetizers at a Fourth of July barbecue or as part of a summer picnic.

Preparation time 55 minutes + 20 minutes cooling + 30 minutes refrigeration
Total cooking time 20 minutes
Serves 4–6

2 tablespoons vegetable oil
I onion, finely chopped
2 cloves garlic, crushed
1 1/2 tablespoons grated fresh ginger
I small red capsicum (pepper), halved, seeded and
    cut into cubes
8 spring onions, finely chopped
480 g (15 oz) white crab meat,
    drained well if frozen
2 teaspoons Tabasco
2 tablespoons chopped fresh flat-leaf parsley
3 tablespoons fresh breadcrumbs
1/2 teaspoon Dijon mustard
I egg, beaten
200 g (6 1/2 oz) seasoned flour, sieved, for coating
100 g (3 1/4 oz) fresh breadcrumbs, for coating
60 g (2 oz) Parmesan, grated, for coating
2 eggs, beaten, for coating
oil, for deep-frying
lemon wedges, to serve

1 Heat the oil in a frying pan and add the onion, garlic and ginger. Cook for 1 minute, then add the capsicum and spring onion and cook for 2 minutes, or until soft. Transfer to a plate and leave for 20 minutes to cool completely. When cool, stir in the crab meat, Tabasco, parsley, breadcrumbs, mustard and some salt and black pepper. Add the egg and bind together.

2 Divide the mixture into 4, 6 or 12, depending on what size cakes you want. Using lightly floured hands and a lightly floured surface, shape into cakes. Place on a tray, cover and refrigerate for 30 minutes, or until firm.

3 Place the flour on a large piece of greaseproof paper. Combine the breadcrumbs and Parmesan on another piece of paper. Place the egg in a shallow dish. One at a time, place the cakes in the flour, then pat off any excess. Place in the egg and use a brush to help coat. Remove with a fish slice, place on the breadcrumbs and Parmesan and toss all over the cake. Reshape the cakes, pressing the crumbs firmly on, then place on a tray.

4 Heat a 1 cm (1/2 inch) depth of oil in a non-stick frying pan and cook the cakes, in batches, over medium heat for 1–2 minutes each side, or until golden. Drain on crumpled paper towels and serve with lemon wedges.

Chef's tip To keep the crab cakes warm and crisp, place on a wire rack in a warm oven.

Seafood risotto

In this recipe, baby clams, prawns, mussels, crab and red mullet provide a host of different textures and flavours set in a creamy saffron risotto. Any combination of fresh seafood could be used instead.

Preparation time **35 minutes**
Total cooking time **1 hour**
Serves 4

150 g (5 oz) baby clams
2 red mullet, about 220–250 g (7–8 oz) each, filleted
   and with skin on but scales removed (see page 63)
150 g (5 oz) raw prawns, shells on
200 ml (6 1/2 fl oz) dry white wine
5 tablespoons olive oil
1 small onion, finely chopped
250 g (8 oz) mussels, scrubbed and beards removed
   (see page 62)
1 bay leaf
1 sprig of fresh thyme
500 ml (16 fl oz) fish stock
pinch of saffron threads
1 clove garlic, finely chopped
250 g (8 oz) arborio rice
60 g (2 oz) Parmesan, grated
grated rind of 1 lime
1 1/2 tablespoons crème fraîche or sour cream
105 g (3 1/2 oz) white crab meat, drained well if frozen
few fresh basil leaves, to garnish

1 Scrub and rinse the clams under running water to get rid of grit, then discard any that are open or damaged. Trim the mullet, then pin bone it following the Chef's techniques on page 63. Shell and devein the prawns, reserving the heads and shells, following the method in the Chef's techniques on page 60.

2 Place the clams in a pan, add half the wine and cook, covered, for 3 minutes, or until they open. Drain through a sieve lined with damp paper towel and reserve the liquid. Discard any unopened clams, then remove the clams from their shells and cover. Discard the shells.

3 In a pan, heat a tablespoon of the oil, add half the onion and cook over low heat for 4 minutes, or until soft and transparent. Add the remaining wine, mussels, bay leaf and thyme and cook, covered, for 2–3 minutes, or until the mussels open. Drain as for the clams, reserving the liquid. Discard any unopened mussels, then remove from their shells and cover.

4 In a pan, place the stock, 500 ml (16 fl oz) water, the clam and mussel liquid, prawn heads and shells and saffron. Bring to the boil, simmer for 10 minutes, then strain through a fine sieve. Return to the rinsed pan and keep warm.

5 In a pan or flameproof casserole, heat a tablespoon of oil, add the garlic and remaining onion and cook over low heat for 2–3 minutes, or until soft. Add the rice and stir for 2 minutes with a wooden spoon, making sure it is completely coated with the oil, then pour in enough stock to just cover the rice. Cook over low heat, stirring continuously, until the stock is absorbed. Continue to cook for 15–20 minutes, pouring in a little stock and allowing it to be absorbed before adding more. The risotto is ready when the rice is just tender but still *al dente* (there should also be a little stock left over). Remove from the heat, fold in the Parmesan, lime rind and crème fraîche and cover. Reserve the remaining stock.

6 Meanwhile, preheat the grill and brush the fish with a little olive oil. Season with salt and black pepper and grill, skin-side-up, for 2 minutes. Cover and keep warm. Heat the remaining oil in a large pan and toss the prawns over high heat for 2 minutes, or until pink and cooked through.

7 Pour the remaining stock into a pan, add the mussels, clams and crab and just heat through. Mix the seafood and its liquid into the risotto and transfer to a serving dish. Place the mullet and basil on top.

Smoked haddock gougère

A cheese-flavoured crown of choux pastry here holds a filling of smoked haddock, leek, tomato and dill. For a variation, you could try a mixture of fish such as salmon, trout or monkfish, or perhaps some shellfish.

Preparation time **35 *minutes***
Total cooking time **45 *minutes***
Serves 6

CHOUX PASTRY
150 g (5 oz) plain flour
100 g (3^1/4 oz) unsalted butter, cut into cubes
pinch of salt
4 eggs, lightly beaten
100 g (3^1/4 oz) Cheddar, coarsely grated
1 teaspoon Dijon mustard

FILLING
310 g (10 oz) smoked haddock fillet
15 g (^{1}/2 oz) unsalted butter
1 small leek or 4 spring onions, white part only, sliced
15 g (^{1}/2 oz) plain flour
180 ml (5^3/4 fl oz) milk
1 large tomato, peeled, seeded and cut into
* 1 cm (^{1}/2 inch) strips*
1 teaspoon chopped fresh dill

1 egg, beaten
1 tablespoon grated Parmesan
1 tablespoon lightly toasted fresh breadcrumbs
20 g (^{3}/4 oz) unsalted butter, melted
fresh dill, to garnish

1 Brush six 14.5 x 3 cm (5^3/4 x 1^1/4 inch) round gratin dishes with melted butter and refrigerate to set.

2 To make the choux pastry, sift the flour onto a clean sheet of greaseproof paper. Place 250 ml (8 fl oz) water, the butter and salt in a pan. Heat until the butter and water come to the boil. Remove from the heat and add the flour all at once, then mix well using a wooden spoon. Return to the heat and stir until a smooth ball forms and the dough leaves the sides of the pan, then remove from the heat and place the dough in a bowl. Using a wooden spoon or electric beaters, add the eggs to the dough a little at a time, beating well after each addition. The mixture is ready to use when it is smooth, thick and glossy. Beat in the cheese, mustard and season well with salt and black pepper. Cover and set aside.

3 To make the filling, place the smoked haddock flat in a shallow pan and pour in enough cold water to cover. Slowly bring to the boil, covered, then turn off the heat and leave for 7 minutes.

4 Melt the butter in a deep pan, add the leek and cook over low heat for 3 minutes to soften. Sprinkle over the flour, stir in using a wooden spoon and cook for 1 minute. Remove from the heat, mix in the milk, then return to the heat and bring to the boil, stirring continuously. Simmer for 1 minute, or until the mixture thickens.

5 Preheat the oven to moderately hot 200°C (400°F/ Gas 6). Lift the fish from its cooking liquid, pat dry with paper towels, then use a fork to lightly take the fish off its skin in flakes. Gently stir the flakes into the filling with the tomato, dill and some salt and black pepper.

6 Fill a piping bag with a 1–1.25 cm (^{1}/2–^{5}/8 inch) nozzle with the pastry. Pipe a circle around the outside of the base of the prepared dishes, then a second circle on top to cover the side of the dish. Spoon the filling into the middle of the choux circles and brush the top of the pastry lightly with the beaten egg. Combine the Parmesan and breadcrumbs, sprinkle over the filling, then drizzle with the melted butter. Place on a baking tray and bake for 15–20 minutes, or until the pastry is risen and crisp. Sprinkle with dill to garnish.

Chef's tips You can also spoon in the pastry to cover the sides of the dish and give a more peaky surface.

To make one large gougère, use a deep 20 cm (8 inch) round ovenproof dish and bake for 30–35 minutes.

Fish and chips

Tradition at its best: firm white fish that flakes at the touch of a fork, cooked in a crisp batter and served with home-made chips. For the best results, make sure that the fish is really fresh and eat piping hot.

*Preparation time **20 minutes + 30 minutes standing***
*Total cooking time **20 minutes***
Serves 4

600 g (1 1/4 lb) floury potatoes, peeled
oil, for deep-frying
4 x 150–180 g (5–5 3/4 oz) pieces firm white
** fish fillet, skinned**
2–3 tablespoons seasoned flour
lemon wedges, to garnish

BATTER
160 g (5 1/4 oz) cornflour
160 g (5 1/4 oz) plain flour
3 teaspoons baking powder
315–500 ml (10–16 fl oz) beer

1 Cut the potatoes into 5–10 mm (1/4–1/2 inch) wide, 1 cm (1/2 inch) deep and 6–8 cm (2 1/2–3 inch) long batons. Place in a bowl and cover with cold water.
2 To make the batter, sift the cornflour, plain flour, baking powder and some salt and black pepper into a bowl and make a well in the centre. Gradually pour in the beer, using a wooden spoon to beat it into the flour, until the mixture becomes a smooth batter the

consistency of cream (the amount of liquid you need will depend on the flour you use). Cover and leave for 30 minutes at room temperature.
3 Meanwhile, fill a deep-fat fryer or heavy-based pan one third full of oil and heat to 160–170°C (315–325°F) (a cube of bread dropped into the oil will brown in 30 seconds). Drain and pat the chips dry, then fry until the bubbles subside and the chips have formed a thin, light-golden skin. Lift out the chips, allowing excess oil to drip back into the fryer, and transfer the chips onto crumpled paper towels.
4 Increase the temperature of the oil to 180°C (350°F) (a cube of bread dropped into the oil will brown in 15 seconds). Wash the fish and dry thoroughly on paper towels. Place the seasoned flour on a plate and coat the fish, shaking off the excess. Dip the fish into the batter until it is evenly coated, then lift out using fingers or forks to allow any excess mixture to drip off. Lower the fish carefully into the fryer or pan and fry, in batches if necessary, for 5 minutes, or until golden and crisp. Do not overcrowd the pan or the temperature will be lowered. Remove and drain on crumpled paper towels. Season with salt, place on a wire rack and keep warm.
5 Place the chips in the oil again and fry until golden and crisp. Remove and drain, season with salt and serve with the fish, lemon wedges and tartare or tomato sauce.

Sole Véronique with potato galettes

A classic French recipe using white grapes in a white wine sauce to accompany poached lemon sole. Here the dish is served on crisp potato galettes.

*Preparation time **1 hour***
*Total cooking time **1 hour 15 minutes***
Serves 4

POTATO GALETTES
500 g (1 lb) floury potatoes, peeled and cut
  into even-sized pieces
4 egg whites
clarified butter or ghee, for frying

8 x 85 g (2³/₄ oz) lemon sole fillets
2 French shallots, finely chopped
100 ml (3¹/₄ fl oz) dry white wine
200 ml (6¹/₂ fl oz) fish stock
200 g (6¹/₂ oz) seedless white grapes
300 ml (10 fl oz) cream

1 To make the potato galettes, place the potatoes in a large pan of salted, cold water. Cover and bring to the boil, then reduce the heat and simmer for about 15–20 minutes, or until the potatoes are tender to the point of a sharp knife. Drain, return to the pan and shake over low heat for 1–2 minutes to remove excess moisture. Mash or push through a fine sieve, season with salt and black pepper and cool.

2 Meanwhile, wash the sole and dry well on paper towels. Fold the skinned side under at each end of the fillets to give eight fillets about 10 cm (4 inches) long. Butter a shallow 30 x 21 cm (12 x 8¹/₂ inch) ovenproof dish and sprinkle half the shallots over the base. Place the sole on the shallots, drizzle with one tablespoon each of the wine and stock and season lightly with some salt and black pepper. Cover with plastic wrap and set aside in the refrigerator.

3 Put the grapes in a pan of boiling water and cook for 15 seconds, then drain and plunge into iced water to cool. Remove from the water, peel away their skins and reserve the grapes and skins separately.

4 Preheat the oven to moderate 180°C (350°F/Gas 4). In a bowl, whisk the egg whites until they hold in stiff peaks. Stir a quarter of the egg white into the potato then, using a spatula or large metal spoon, gently fold in the remaining egg white.

5 Place a 1 cm (¹/₂ inch) depth of clarified butter or ghee in a large heavy-based frying pan and place over moderate heat. Lightly oil the inside of an 8 cm (3 inch) round plain pastry cutter and place it in the pan. Place a 5 mm (¹/₄ inch) layer of the potato inside the cutter. Gently loosen around the sides with a palette knife and lift the cutter away. Repeat to fill the pan, leaving enough space between the galettes to turn them. Fry for 5 minutes each side, or until golden brown. Drain on crumpled paper towels, then remove to a wire rack in a low oven and keep warm.

6 Place the remaining shallots, wine and stock in a pan. Add the grape skins, bring to the boil, then simmer for 20 minutes, or until the mixture is syrupy. Meanwhile, bake the sole for 10–12 minutes, or until opaque and cooked through. Stir the cream into the sauce and simmer for 5 minutes, or until syrupy, then strain into a clean pan, discarding the grape skins. Strain the cooking liquid from the fish into the sauce, reduce again to syrupy, then add the grapes and warm through.

7 To serve, place a galette on each plate, arrange two sole fillets on top and coat with the sauce.

Chef's tip For a richer finish, mix together 3 tablespoons lightly whipped cream and 1 egg yolk. Coat the sauced fillets with the mixture, then grill to golden brown.

Smoked salmon and leek terrine with sauce verte

Beautifully light but with a good depth of flavour, this dish makes a perfect appetizer or lunch. Cooking the leeks in fish stock helps them to press together and makes it easier to slice the terrine.

*Preparation time **1 hour + 4 hours refrigeration***
*Total cooking time **20 minutes***
Serves 10

1.5 litres fish stock
30 very small whole leeks, trimmed of tough
  green leaves and roots
10–15 large spinach leaves, stalks removed
560 g (1 lb 2 oz) long slices of smoked salmon
rocket leaves, to garnish

SAUCE VERTE
105 g (3 1/2 oz) watercress, tough stems removed
45 g (1 1/2 oz) fresh chervil leaves, chopped
45 g (1 1/2 oz) fresh dill leaves, chopped
45 g (1 1/2 oz) fresh parsley
few drops of lemon juice
350 ml (11 fl oz) crème fraîche or sour cream

1 In a large pan, bring the fish stock to the boil. Place the leeks in stock, reduce the temperature and gently simmer for 20 minutes, or until tender. Drain well, then set aside to cool.

2 Blanch the spinach in boiling water for 30 seconds. Drain, then plunge into iced water. Carefully lift the leaves out individually and place on paper towels or a cloth and pat dry.

3 Line a 1-litre, 21 x 10 cm (8 1/2 x 4 inch) terrine mould with plastic wrap, then line the base and sides with some of the smoked salmon, allowing a long overhang at one end. Add a layer of spinach, allowing for an overlap over one side of the terrine.

4 Tightly pack two layers of leeks lengthways into the bottom of the lined terrine and season well, then add a layer of half the remaining salmon, followed by one layer of leeks and seasoning. Cover with the remaining salmon and top this with two layers of leeks and seasoning. Fold over the salmon and spinach overhangs to enclose the filling and cover with plastic wrap. Cut a piece of cardboard to fit inside the terrine, cover it twice with foil and place a 1 kg (2 lb) weight on top (this can be cans). Refrigerate for 4 hours.

5 To prepare the sauce verte, place the watercress, herbs and a little water into a blender and blend to a fine purée. Push through a coarse sieve, add the lemon juice and salt and black pepper and fold in the crème fraîche. Cover with plastic wrap and place in the refrigerator until ready to serve.

6 To serve, slice the terrine and arrange on plates with a spoonful of the sauce verte and some rocket leaves to garnish.

Fish minestrone with pesto

A twist on the classic Italian soup, with the addition of scallops, prawns and a dash of cream. The pesto is stirred through at the end and any extra can be tossed through pasta for a great midweek dinner.

*Preparation time **1 hour 15 minutes***
*Total cooking time **15 minutes***
Serves 4

4 fresh scallops
12 tiger prawns, shells on
1 litre fish stock
2¹/₂ tablespoons olive oil
1 small onion, finely diced
1 small carrot, diced
¹/₂ swede, diced
1 small turnip, diced
1 potato, diced
¹/₄ celeriac, diced
50 g (1³/₄ oz) small pasta shapes,
  such as ditalini
25 g (³/₄ oz) French beans, cut into
  5 mm (¹/₄ inch) lengths
1 zucchini (courgette), diced
3 tablespoons cream
50 g (1³/₄ oz) cooked or canned flageolet beans
few sprigs of fresh chervil, to garnish

PESTO
55 g (1³/₄ oz) garlic
55 g (1³/₄ oz) pine kernels, toasted
35 g (1¹/₄ oz) grated Parmesan
30 g (1 oz) fresh basil leaves
45 g (1¹/₂ oz) fresh parsley leaves
200 ml (6¹/₂ fl oz) olive oil

1 To prepare the scallops, follow the method in the Chef's techniques on page 62. Place the scallops flat on a board and slice each one into three circles, leaving the orange roe whole. Shell and devein the prawns, following the method in the Chef's techniques on page 60. Cover and refrigerate until needed.

2 To make the pesto, put all the ingredients in a blender or food processor and blend to a smooth thick mixture. Transfer to a clean screw-top jar and cover the surface with a layer of oil to stop it oxidizing.

3 Place the stock in a small pan and bring to the boil. Heat the oil in a large pan, add the onion, carrot and swede, cover and cook over low heat for 2 minutes, or until soft and translucent. Add the turnip and potato, pour in the boiling stock, season lightly with salt and bring to the boil. Add the celeriac and pasta and simmer for 5 minutes, or until the vegetables are just tender. Add the beans and zucchini and cook for 2 minutes.

4 Remove from the heat and stir in the cream and flageolet beans. Add 3 tablespoons of the pesto, the scallops and prawns and mix gently to blend in the pesto. Season with salt and black pepper, then return to the stove just to bring back to the boil (do not continue to cook or the scallops and prawns will overcook and toughen). Garnish with chervil sprigs to serve.

Chef's tip Leftover pesto will keep in the refrigerator for up to one week or it can be stored in the freezer in an airtight container. Toss with pasta, use as a salad dressing or place on cooked mussels in the half shell and quickly grill until bubbling.

Creamy and salsa oysters

Two versions of classic oyster dishes. The creamy version is made with cream, white wine and bacon and is flashed under the grill to give a golden topping. If you prefer less heat, just omit the chilli. The salsa oysters are not cooked and come with a fiery tomato, red onion and lime dressing.

Preparation time **50 minutes**
Total cooking time **15 minutes (Creamy)**
Serves 4

24 oysters

CREAMY
2 teaspoons Tabasco
120 g (4 oz) bacon rashers, rind removed
4 egg yolks
100 ml (3 1/4 fl oz) white wine
80 ml (2 3/4 fl oz) thick (double) cream,
 lightly whipped
1/2 red chilli, seeded and finely chopped
1 tablespoon olive oil
1 small red capsicum (pepper), cut into matchsticks

OR

SALSA
410 g (13 oz) ripe tomatoes, peeled, seeded
 and diced
1 red onion, finely chopped
juice of 2 limes
1 teaspoon Tabasco
1 teaspoon roughly chopped fresh coriander
3 teaspoons roughly chopped fresh flat-leaf parsley
fresh coriander leaves, to garnish

1 Shuck the oysters following the method in the Chef's techniques on page 60. Add the oysters to their liquid in the bowl and refrigerate. Clean the deeper half of the shells thoroughly and discard the flat halves.

2 To make the creamy oysters, add half the Tabasco to the oysters before refrigerating. Place the bacon in a small pan, cover with cold water, bring to the boil and simmer for 4 minutes. Drain, then run under cold water to remove excess salt. Tip the bacon onto paper towels to drain, then cut into matchsticks.

3 Place the egg yolks, wine and remaining Tabasco in a heatproof bowl over a pan of simmering water, ensuring the bowl is not touching the water. Whisk vigorously until the mixture has increased to three or four times the original volume and leaves a trail across the surface when lifted on the whisk. Remove the bowl from the pan, whisk until it cools to room temperature, then fold in the cream and chilli and set aside.

4 Preheat the grill. Heat the oil in a pan and fry the bacon until golden, then add the capsicum and cook over medium heat for 1 minute, or until soft but not coloured. Heat the oysters and their juices in another pan over low heat for 1 minute. Do not overheat or the oysters will toughen. Put the warm oysters back in their shells and place in an ovenproof dish (a layer of rock salt underneath will help them stay balanced). Pour over the juices and place the bacon and capsicum mixture on top. Spoon the egg mixture over and place under the grill for 2 minutes, or until golden. Serve immediately.

5 To make the salsa, mix together all the ingredients except the whole coriander leaves with some salt and black pepper. Cover with plastic wrap and set aside for 20 minutes at room temperature. Place an oyster in each shell and spoon over some juices and a little salsa, then garnish with a coriander leaf. Arrange on a bed of salad leaves or crushed ice.

Creamy oysters (top) and Salsa oysters

Spaghetti marinara

Meaning 'Mariner's style', the name of this pasta dish originated from fishermen's wives throwing their husbands' daily catch into a quick tomato, garlic, herb and olive oil sauce.

*Preparation time **35 minutes***
*Total cooking time **50 minutes***
Serves 4

3 tablespoons olive oil
I onion, finely chopped
2 cloves garlic, crushed
I tablespoon tomato paste
2 x 400 g (12³/4 oz) cans chopped tomatoes
2 sprigs of fresh thyme
I bay leaf
250 g (8 oz) fresh tuna, skinned and cut
  into 2 cm (³/4 inch) cubes
250 g (8 oz) squid tubes, sliced into 5 mm
  (¹/4 inch) rings
250 g (8 oz) white crab meat, drained
  well if frozen
4 tablespoons chopped fresh basil leaves
500 g (I lb) spaghetti

1 In a large pan, heat 2 tablespoons of the olive oil, add the onion and garlic and cook for 4 minutes, or until the onion is soft and translucent. Stir in the tomato paste and cook for a further minute. Add the tomatoes, thyme and bay leaf, season with salt and black pepper, then bring to the boil, lower the heat and simmer for about 25 minutes.

2 Heat the remaining oil in a large frying pan, add the tuna and toss over high heat for about 3 minutes, or until lightly cooked. Lift out the tuna using a slotted spoon and drain in a colander over a bowl. Reheat the oil remaining in the pan, add the squid rings and toss over high heat for 3 minutes, or until opaque, then remove and add to the tuna to drain.

3 Remove and discard the thyme and bay leaf from the tomato sauce, then add the tuna, squid, crab meat and 3 tablespoons of the basil. Stir gently to combine without breaking up the fish and season with salt and black pepper. Remove from the heat and keep warm.

4 Meanwhile, bring a large pan of salted water to the boil. Add a splash of oil to stop the pasta sticking and cook the spaghetti according to the manufacturer's instructions. Drain well.

5 Serve the spaghetti on warm plates and spoon the marinara sauce on top. Sprinkle with the remaining basil and serve immediately.

Chef's tip Frying the seafood at a high temperature will seal it, give a good flavour and allow it to hold its shape.

'Lasagne' of salmon with tomato and spinach

There is no pasta in this special dish, but the effect is like a lasagne, with layers of pink salmon, dark-green spinach leaves, white and tomato sauces making for a stunning dinner-party recipe.

Preparation time **1 hour**
Total cooking time **1 hour 15 minutes**
Serves 4

4 x 150 g (5 oz) thick centre cuts of fresh salmon fillet, skinned and cut into 3 slices horizontally (ask your fishmonger to do this)
90 ml (3 fl oz) olive oil
2 onions, finely chopped
1 kg (2 lb) ripe tomatoes, peeled, seeded and diced
2 cloves garlic, crushed
bouquet garni (see Chef's tip)
45 g (1 1/2 oz) unsalted butter
750 g (1 1/2 lb) fresh spinach
a small pinch of nutmeg
12 small black olives, halved and pitted, to garnish
few sprigs of fresh chervil, to garnish

BEURRE BLANC
3 French shallots, finely chopped
315 ml (10 fl oz) white wine
3 tablespoons cider vinegar
1 tablespoon thick (double) cream or crème fraîche
180 g (5 3/4 oz) unsalted butter, cut into small cubes and chilled
2 tablespoons finely chopped fresh chives

WHITE SAUCE
15 g (1/2 oz) unsalted butter
15 g (1/2 oz) plain flour
250 ml (8 fl oz) milk

1 Separate the slices of salmon, brush with olive oil, cover and place in the refrigerator. Heat the oil in a pan, add the onion, cover and cook for 4 minutes, or until soft and translucent. Stir in the tomato, garlic, bouquet garni and some salt and black pepper. Cook for about 40 minutes, stirring occasionally, until the mixture is thick. Discard the bouquet garni, re-season and keep warm.

2 To make the beurre blanc, place the shallots, wine and vinegar in a pan, bring to the boil and cook to reduce by a quarter. Add the cream and remove from the heat, then whisk in the butter a piece at a time until you have a creamy, flowing sauce that coats the back of a spoon. Strain into a bowl, stir in the chives, cover with plastic wrap and sit over a pan of warm water.

3 To make the white sauce, melt the butter in a heavy-based pan over low-medium heat. Sprinkle the flour over the butter and cook for 1–2 minutes without allowing it to colour, stirring continuously with a wooden spoon. Remove the pan from the heat and slowly add the milk, whisking to avoid lumps. Return to medium heat and bring to the boil, stirring constantly. Cook for 3–4 minutes, or until the sauce coats the back of a spoon. Cover and keep warm. Preheat the grill.

4 Melt the butter in a large frying pan or wok, add the spinach and toss over high heat for 2 minutes, or until wilted. Add the nutmeg, salt and black pepper and place in a sieve over a bowl to allow the moisture to drain through. Season the fish and grill for 1 minute each side.

5 To serve, take four plates and place a salmon slice on each one. Using half the spinach, spread a layer on each slice, then add half the white sauce, followed by half the tomato sauce. Cover with another slice of fish, the remaining spinach, white and tomato sauce, and finish with the remaining salmon. Spoon the beurre blanc around the base of the plate and garnish with the olive halves and chervil leaves.

Chef's tip To make a bouquet garni, wrap the green part of a leek loosely around a bay leaf, a sprig of thyme, some celery leaves and a few stalks of parsley, then tie with string, leaving a long tail for easy removal.

Snapper with fennel en papillote

Cooked in a parcel of greaseproof paper or foil to retain all the juices and flavours, the white wine, basil leaves and gentle anise flavour of fennel infuse the sweet snapper or mullet.

Preparation time **40 minutes**
Total cooking time **35 minutes**
Serves 4

2 x 400 g (12³/4 oz) snapper or red mullet,
  filleted (see page 63)
2 large fennel bulbs
60 g (2 oz) unsalted butter
16 fresh basil leaves
80 ml (2³/4 fl oz) white wine
4 teaspoons Pastis or Ricard (optional)

1 Wash the fish, dry on paper towels and refrigerate until needed. With a small sharp knife, trim off the small stalks at the top of the fennel bulbs, keeping the leaves and discarding the thick stalks. With a large sharp knife, cut the bulb in half from the top down through the root, then cut away and discard the root. Cut the fennel into 5 mm (1/4 inch) thick slices.

2 Heat the butter in a pan, add the fennel, cover and cook over low heat for 25 minutes, or until soft to the point of a sharp knife. Remove from the stove and season with salt and black pepper. Preheat the oven to hot 220°C (425°F/Gas 7).

3 Fold a piece of greaseproof paper or foil in two, then cut out a large half tear-drop shape, 5 cm (2 inches) bigger than the fish. Open the paper or foil out and you should have a heart shape. Repeat to make four in total, then lay the shapes flat and brush with melted butter. Spoon the fennel onto one side of each heart and spread to the size of the fish. Place a fish fillet on top and lightly season with salt and black pepper. Arrange four basil leaves on each piece of fish, then sprinkle each one with a tablespoon of white wine and a teaspoon of Pastis or Ricard. Top with the reserved sprigs of fennel leaf.

4 Immediately fold the empty side of paper or foil over the fish and seal the edges by twisting and folding tightly. Place on a baking tray or in a shallow ovenproof dish and bake for 5–8 minutes.

5 Place the parcels on plates and allow your guests to open them and release the aromas.

Chef's tip Other fish can be cooked by this method, such as perch, mackerel or cod. The cooking times will vary according to the thickness and shape of the fish.

Thai green fish curry

This fish curry is prepared with an easy-to-make home-made green curry paste, which gives a fresh, authentic Thai taste. Serve with steamed jasmine fragrant rice.

Preparation time **15 minutes**
Total cooking time **20 minutes**
Serves 4–6

GREEN CURRY PASTE
250 g (8 oz) coconut milk
8 small green chillies (bird's-eye), halved and seeded
1 stalk lemon grass, chopped
2 tablespoons lime juice
25 g ($^3/4$ oz) galangal or ginger, sliced
1 teaspoon ground coriander
$^1/2$ teaspoon ground cumin
5 Asian shallots or spring onions, peeled and chopped
3 kaffir lime leaves, chopped

1 tablespoon sunflower oil
**$^1/2$ mild red or green chilli, seeded and
  cut into shreds**
**25 g ($^3/4$ oz) drained green peppercorns in brine,
  plus 1 teaspoon of brine**
1 teaspoon sugar
400 ml (12$^3/4$ fl oz) can coconut milk
5 kaffir lime leaves
**750 g (1$^1/2$ lb) firm white fish fillets, skinned
  and cut into 4 cm (1$^1/2$ inch) cubes**

1 tablespoon fish sauce
2 tablespoons roughly torn basil leaves, for garnish

1 To make the green curry paste, blend all the ingredients in a blender or food processor, scraping down the sides of the bowl occasionally, until the mixture is smooth and forms a thick paste. If it is too thick, add a little more coconut milk or a few drops of sunflower oil. Place in a bowl, cover and set aside.

2 In a wok or large frying pan, heat the sunflower oil, then add the chilli and toss for about 4 minutes, or until lightly golden. Add the peppercorns, brine, sugar and coconut milk, bring to the boil and simmer for about 3 minutes.

3 Add 4 tablespoons of the green curry paste, the lime leaves and the fish. Simmer for 5–10 minutes, or until the fish is cooked. Remove and discard the lime leaves, season with salt, black pepper and the fish sauce and keep warm.

4 To serve, lift out the fish into a warm serving dish and spoon the sauce over. Sprinkle with the basil and serve with steamed jasmine rice.

Chef's tip The leftover curry paste can be stored in an airtight container in the freezer and used to make a fish, chicken or vegetable green curry.

Seafood pie

A classic family dish, this seafood pie is made with white fish, mussels and prawns in a light wine sauce, topped with a purée of potato that is baked to lightly golden in the oven.

*Preparation time **50 minutes***
*Total cooking time **1 hour 10 minutes***
Serves 6

500 g (1 lb) mussels, scrubbed and beards removed
  (see page 62)
150 g (5 oz) raw prawns, shells on
60 g (2 oz) unsalted butter
2 French shallots, finely chopped
1 leek, white part only, cut into julienne strips
  (see Chef's tips)
220 ml (7 fl oz) dry white wine
500 ml (16 fl oz) milk
1 onion, studded with 1 clove
bouquet garni (see Chef's tips)
600 g (1 1/4 lb) mixed firm white fish fillets, such
  as lemon sole, plaice, cod and halibut, skinned
  and cut into 3 cm (1 1/4 inch) cubes
30 g (1 oz) plain flour
1 kg (2 lb) floury potatoes, peeled and cut into pieces
50 g (1 3/4 oz) unsalted butter, extra
1 egg yolk
4 tablespoons cream
small pinch of ground nutmeg

1 Place the mussels in a cool place covered with a damp cloth. Shell and devein the prawns, following the method in the Chef's techniques on page 60.
2 In a pan, melt half the butter over low heat, then add the shallots, cover and cook for 2–3 minutes, or until soft. Add the leek and cook for 2 minutes, uncovered, then add a tablespoon of the wine and simmer until the liquid has evaporated. Place the mixture in a shallow oval 28 x 20 cm (11 x 8 inch) ovenproof dish.
3 Place the mussels and remaining wine in a pan, bring slowly to the boil, covered, and cook for 2–3 minutes, or until all the mussels are open. Discard any unopened mussels. Drain, reserving the cooking liquid, then remove the mussels from their shells and scatter into the dish. Strain the liquid through a sieve lined with muslin or a damp piece of paper towel and set aside.
4 Add the milk, onion and bouquet garni to a pan, bring to barely simmering and cook for 5 minutes. Remove the onion and bouquet garni and add the fish, prawns and reserved mussel liquid. Heat to just simmering and poach the seafood for 2 minutes. Drain, reserving the liquid and keeping it hot, and add the seafood to the dish.
5 Melt the remaining butter in a pan over low heat, sprinkle over the flour and cook, stirring, for 1 minute without colouring. Remove from the heat and blend in the hot poaching liquid. Return to medium heat, bring to the boil, stirring constantly, and cook for 3–4 minutes, or until it thickens and coats the back of a spoon. Season, then pour over the fish. Cover and refrigerate.
6 Preheat the oven to moderate 180°C (350°F/Gas 4). Place the potatoes in a pan of salted, cold water, cover and bring to the boil, then reduce the heat and simmer for 15–20 minutes, or until the potatoes are tender to a sharp knife. Drain, return to the pan and shake over low heat for 1–2 minutes to remove excess moisture. Mash or push through a fine sieve back into the pan, then beat in the extra butter, yolk and finally the cream. Season with nutmeg, salt and black pepper, spoon into a piping bag with a large star nozzle and pipe a pattern over the surface of the fish, or spread the potato, then use a fork to peak it. Bake for 30 minutes, or until lightly golden.

Chef's tips Julienne strips are strips of vegetables, the size and shape of matchsticks.

To make a bouquet garni, wrap the green part of a leek loosely around a bay leaf, a sprig of thyme, some celery leaves and a few stalks of parsley, then tie with string, leaving a long tail for easy removal.

Seafood gumbo

A thick, spicy soup from the American South with its origins in Creole cuisine, influenced by African and French cooking. The original meaning of 'Gumbo' was okra, and this vegetable is what thickens the dish.

*Preparation time **45 minutes***
*Total cooking time **35 minutes***
Serves 4

12 tiger prawns, shells on
50 g (1³/4 oz) long-grain rice
2¹/2 tablespoons vegetable oil
2 large onions, chopped
1 celery stick, finely chopped
2 cloves garlic, crushed
1 red capsicum (pepper), diced
1 green capsicum (pepper), diced
3 tablespoons tomato paste
1 litre fish stock
2 teaspoons chopped fresh oregano
1 cooked crab in its shell, cleaned and cut
  into quarters or 4 cooked crab claws
  in their shells (see Chef's tip)
250 g (8 oz) okra, cut into 1 cm (¹/2 inch)
  round slices
150 g (5 oz) snapper or red mullet fillet, skinned
  and cut into 4 cm (1¹/2 inch) pieces
1 teaspoon Tabasco
1 teaspoon Worcestershire sauce
2 spring onions, finely chopped

1 Shell and devein the tiger prawns, leaving the tails intact, following the method in the Chef's techniques on page 60. Cook the rice in boiling salted water for 10 minutes, or until tender, drain and leave to cool.

2 In a large frying pan, heat the oil. Add the onion, celery, garlic and capsicum. Stir over medium heat for 5 minutes, or until soft but not coloured. Mix in the tomato paste and stir for 1 minute, then add the stock, oregano and crab and simmer for 5 minutes. Gently stir in the okra, season lightly, cover and simmer for 15–20 minutes, or until the okra is tender.

3 Remove the pan from the stove and lift out the crab pieces, crack them with the base of a small heavy pan, and remove the meat as whole pieces if possible. Discard the shells, cover the crab meat and keep warm.

4 Skim the gumbo to remove any oil or foam, then return to the stove, add the fish and prawns and simmer for 2 minutes. Add the Tabasco and Worcestershire sauces, stir in the rice and bring the gumbo back to simmering. Taste and add more salt, pepper or sauces if necessary (the soup should have a good hint of chilli). To serve, ladle into bowls and garnish with spring onion. Serve with bread.

Chef' tip To clean a crab, remove the stomach sac and grey spongy fingers (gills).

52 *seafood*

Lobster américaine

One of the most famous of all lobster dishes, where the lobster is cooked on the shell in a rich tomato and wine sauce. There is much dispute on the origins of the name—whether it should be 'Armoricaine', the ancient name for Brittany in France, or 'Américaine', after a French chef who had worked in America.

*Preparation time **30 minutes***
*Total cooking time **50 minutes***
Serves 4

4 x 500 g (1 lb) lobsters or 2 x 800 g–1 kg
* (1 lb 10 oz–2 lb) lobsters*
100 ml (3¼ fl oz) vegetable oil
45 g (1½ oz) unsalted butter
1 onion, diced
1 carrot, diced
2 celery sticks, diced
150 ml (5 fl oz) dry white wine
2½ tablespoons brandy
500 ml (16 fl oz) fish stock
3 tablespoons tomato paste
500 g (1 lb) ripe tomatoes, halved and seeded
1 bouquet garni (see Chef's tips)
fresh parsley, to garnish

1 If you have bought live lobsters, kill them according to the method in the Chef's techniques on page 61. If you prefer not to do this, ask your fishmonger to do it.
2 Prepare the lobster following the method in the Chef's techniques on page 61. To fry the lobster claws and tails, heat the oil in a large frying pan and add the claws and tails. Fry quickly, turning with long-handled tongs, until they change colour from blue to red and the tail flesh shrinks visibly from the shell. Lift them out of the pan onto a plate and continue to prepare the lobster according to the method on page 61.
3 Heat half the butter in the pan and fry the pieces of head shell quickly until the colour has changed, as before. Remove any flesh and set aside. Add the reserved shell from the tail with the onion, carrot and celery and cook for about 5 minutes, or until lightly brown. Add the wine and reduce by half before adding the brandy and stock. Stir in the tomato paste and cook for 1 minute before adding the tomato halves. Cover the pan with a lid and, over gentle heat, cook for 20 minutes, or until the tomatoes are pulpy. While this is cooking, place the reserved coral and tomalley into a blender with the remaining butter and blend until smooth.
4 Remove the lid from the pan, add the bouquet garni and the reserved fried claws and cook for 10 minutes. Lift out the claws and cool before cracking to remove the flesh.
5 Strain the tomato mixture through a sieve into a clean pan, discarding the shell, tomato skins, bouquet garni and diced vegetables. Cook the tomato mixture, stirring occasionally, for 4 minutes, or until lightly syrupy.
6 Whisk the coral and tomalley flavoured butter into the sauce until smooth, then add the lobster tail flesh and simmer very gently for 1 minute (if overcooked, the flesh with be tough). Remove the pan from the stove and leave the lobster tail to rest for 5 minutes in the sauce before removing and slicing into round slices. Gently rewarm the slices in the sauce with all the cracked claw and head meat. To serve, spoon onto hot plates and garnish with the parsley.

Chef's tips To make a bouquet garni, wrap the green part of a leek loosely around a bay leaf, a sprig of thyme, some celery leaves and a few stalks of parsley, then tie with string, leaving a long tail for easy removal.

Lobsters generally have two large front claws. Although in some countries crayfish are also called lobsters, they do not have the large front claws.

Sole meunière

A stylish classic: the sole is quickly pan-fried, then butter and lemon juice is poured over and the fish is eaten hot with parsley and lemon wedges. Dover sole is recommended for its firm texture and succulence, but any flat fish could be substituted.

*Total preparation time **10 minutes***
*Total cooking time **10 minutes***
Serves 4

4 sole fillets, about 180–200 g
  (5³/4-6¹/2 oz) each, skinned
100 g (3¹/4 oz) clarified butter or ghee
100 g (3¹/4 oz) seasoned flour
100 g (3¹/4 oz) unsalted butter, chilled and
  cut into cubes
1 tablespoon lemon juice, strained
2 teaspoons finely chopped fresh parsley,
  to garnish
1 lemon, cut into wedges, to garnish

1 Wash the fish, then dry well on paper towels. In a large frying pan, heat the clarified butter until hot.

2 Place the seasoned flour on a plate and roll the fillets in it to coat thoroughly, then pat off any excess. Place in the pan, skinned-side-up, and fry for about 2 minutes, turning once, or until lightly golden. Remove and place on hot plates.

3 Drain off the hot butter used for frying and wipe out the pan with paper towels before returning to the heat. Add the butter to the pan and cook until golden and frothy. Remove from the stove, immediately add the lemon juice and, while still bubbling, spoon or pour over the fish.

4 Garnish with some parsley and serve immediately with the lemon wedges.

Basque-style tuna

Typically this Basque dish contains capsicums, onions, tomatoes and ham—ideal ingredients to match the meaty texture of fresh tuna.

*Total preparation time **1 hour 5 minutes***
*Total cooking time **20 minutes***
Serves 4

250 g (8 oz) ripe tomatoes
3 tablespoons olive oil
15 g ($^1/_2$ oz) unsalted butter
4 x 185 g (6 oz) pieces tuna, skinned
2 onions, thinly sliced
1 small red capsicum (pepper), thinly sliced
1 small yellow capsicum (pepper), thinly sliced
1 small green capsicum (pepper), thinly sliced
3 cloves garlic, finely chopped
155 ml (5 fl oz) dry white wine
1 bouquet garni (see Chef's tip)
155 g (5 oz) Bayonne or Parma ham, thinly sliced and cut into 3 cm (1$^1/_4$ inch) pieces
$^1/_2$ tablespoon chopped fresh parsley, to garnish

1 Bring a small pan of water to the boil. With the point of a sharp knife, score a small cross on the skin at the base of each tomato. Drop into the boiling water for 10 seconds, then plunge into a bowl of iced water. Peel the skin away from the cross, then cut around and remove the stalk. Cut the tomatoes into quarters and discard the seeds. Roughly chop the tomato flesh.

2 In a large frying pan, heat 2 tablespoons of the oil and the butter. When foaming, add the tuna and fry over high heat for 1 minute each side, or until lightly golden. Remove from the pan. Add the onion, cover and cook over low heat, stirring occasionally, for 3–4 minutes, or until soft but not coloured. Add the capsicum and garlic and cook gently for 1 minute, or until soft. Return the fish to the pan, add the tomato, wine, bouquet garni and some salt. Cover and simmer for 5 minutes.

3 Remove the tuna and cover with foil to keep warm. Bring the mixture in the pan to the boil and cook rapidly to reduce for about 5 minutes, or until the liquid lightly coats the back of a spoon. Season with black pepper and a little more salt if necessary. Heat the remaining oil in a frying pan, add the ham and quickly fry for about 10 seconds each side (you may need to do this in batches, adding a little extra oil if necessary).

4 To serve, place the fish on plates and spoon the vegetable mixture over. Scatter the ham over or around the fish and sprinkle with the parsley.

Chef's tip To make a bouquet garni, wrap the green part of a leek loosely around a bay leaf, a sprig of thyme, some celery leaves and a few stalks of parsley, then tie with string, leaving a long tail for easy removal.

Chef's techniques

◆

Shucking oysters

Use a shucker with a protection shield and always protect the hand holding the oyster with a thick cloth.

Scrub the oysters in cold water. Place an oyster, rounded-side-down, on a thick doubled cloth in the palm of your hand.

Insert an oyster knife through the pointed end of the oyster at the hinge where the top and bottom shells meet. Work the knife in until at least 3 cm (1 1/4 inches) is inside. Twist the knife to separate the shells.

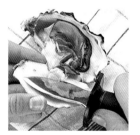

Slide the knife between the oyster and the top shell, cut through the hinge muscle and remove the top shell.

Slide the knife between the oyster and the bottom shell to release it. Remove the oyster and tip any liquid through a muslin-lined sieve into a bowl to get rid of any sand. Reserve the liquid.

Preparing prawns

If using raw prawns, remove the dark intestinal vein, which is unpleasant to eat.

Peel off the shell, being careful to keep the flesh intact. Leave the tail end intact if specified in the recipe.

Make a shallow cut along the back of the prawn with a small knife to expose the dark intestinal vein.

Remove the vein with the tip of a knife and discard. Rinse the prawns and pat dry with paper towels.

Preparing lobster bisque

The shell is an important part of the flavouring for this soup and is cooked with the meat.

Cut the lobsters in half lengthways. Remove and discard the sac in the head and the vein down the centre of the tail.

Twist off the claws and bat them with a rolling pin or the base of a small heavy pan to crack them.

Using a large sharp knife, cut across the tail into three or four pieces.

Killing a lobster

Place the lobster in the freezer for about 2 hours to desensitize it.

Hold the lobster tail down under a heavy cloth. Using a large sharp knife, place the point in the centre of the head and quickly pierce right through to the board, cutting down and forward between the eyes.

Preparing lobster américaine

Depending on the type of lobster you have, the claws will vary in size.

Twist and remove the two main claws, if applicable, from where they meet the body. Separate the head from the tail. Cook the claws and tail according to the method in the recipe.

Remove the flesh from the tail by snipping with scissors around the edge of the flat undershell and lifting it away.

Gently ease the flesh out of the tail in one piece using your fingers. Reserve the shell.

With a large sharp knife, split the head in two lengthways. Remove and reserve any coral (roe) and green-grey tomalley (liver). Discard the stomach sac found behind the mouth. Chop the head shell into large pieces.

seafood **61**

Cleaning mussels

Mussels must be very carefully cleaned and should be stored in the refrigerator under a damp cloth.

Clean the mussels by scrubbing the shells with a brush to remove any sand. Scrape the barnacles off with a knife.

Pull off any beards from the mussels.

Discard any mussels that are broken, are not tightly closed or do not close when lightly tapped on a work surface.

Filleting flat fish

Filleting your own fish is simple when you know how—just use a good sharp knife.

Lay the fish dark-side-up. Cut around the outside of the fish with a filleting knife where the flesh meets the fins.

Cut down the centre of the fish from head to tail with a sharp knife. Make sure you cut all the way through to the bone.

Working from the centre of the fillet to the edge, cut away one fillet with long broad strokes of the knife, without leaving too much flesh. Remove the other fillet in the same way, then turn the fish over and repeat.

Cleaning scallops

If the scallops are in their shells, remove them by sliding a knife under the white muscle and orange roe.

Wash the scallops to remove any grit or sand, then pull away the small tough shiny white muscle and the black vein, leaving the orange roe intact.

Skinning fish

The angle of the knife against the skin is most important and skinning will then be easy.

Lay the fillet skin-side-down and cut across the flesh at the tail. Dip your fingers in salt to get a good grip, grasp the tail and, starting at the cut, work the knife away from you at a shallow angle using a sawing action.

Filleting round fish

Choose the freshest fish and fillet them yourself to be sure of the best-quality cut.

Cut off the fins and cut out the gills behind the head and discard.

Make a small cut at the bottom of the stomach, then cut along the underside, stopping just below the gills. Pull the innards out and discard. Rinse the inside of the fish out.

Make a cut around the back of the head, then working from head to tail, cut along the backbone. Holding the knife flat, use long strokes to cut away the flesh, then pull the flesh away from the bones.

Pin boning fish

Salmon or other fish, such as red mullet, often have small bones left in them. These need to be removed.

Run the fingers of your hand along the flesh, pressing lightly to find the bones. Remove any fine pin bones using a pair of tweezers or your fingers.

Serving a salmon

Place the cooked salmon on a piece of greaseproof paper before you begin.

Using a sharp knife, cut the skin just above the tail, then cut through the skin along the back and in front of the gills. Using the knife to help you, work from head to tail to peel off and discard the skin.

Place a serving plate under one side of the greaseproof paper and flip the fish over onto the plate, using the paper to help you. Remove the rest of the skin. Remove the head if preferred.

Scrape away any dark flesh with a knife. Split down the centre of the top fillet, then carefully remove and lay the two quarter fillets each side of the salmon.

Lift out the backbone by peeling it back from the head end. Snip it with scissors just before the tail. Remove any other stray bones and lift up and replace the two fillets.

Published in 1999 by Merehurst Limited, Ferry House, 51–57 Lacy Road, Putney, London SW15 1PR.

Merehurst Limited, Murdoch Books and Le Cordon Bleu thank the 32 masterchefs of all the Le Cordon Bleu Schools, whose knowledge and expertise have made this book possible, especially: Chef Terrien, Chef Boucheret, Chef Duchêne (MOF), Chef Guillut, Chef Pinaud, Paris; Chef Males, Chef Walsh, Chef Power, Chef Neveu, Chef Paton, Chef Poole-Gleed, Chef Wavrin, London; Chef Chantefort, Chef Nicaud, Chef Jambert, Chef Honda, Tokyo; Chef Salambien, Chef Boutin, Chef Harris, Sydney; Chef Lawes, Adelaide; Chef Guiet, Chef Denis, Chef Petibon, Chef Jean Michel Poncet, Ottawa. Of the many students who helped the Chefs test each recipe, a special mention to graduates Hollace Hamilton and Alice Buckley. A very special acknowledgment to Helen Barnard, Alison Oakervee and Deepika Sukhwani, who have been responsible for the coordination of the Le Cordon Bleu team throughout this series under the Presidency of André Cointreau.

Series Manager: Kay Halsey
Series Concept, Design and Art Direction: Juliet Cohen
Food Editor: Lulu Grimes
Designer: Michelle Cutler
Photographer: Joe Filshie
Food Stylist: Carolyn Fienberg
Food Preparation: Justine Poole
Chef's Techniques Photographer: Reg Morrison
Home Economists: Anna Beaumont, Michaela Le Compte, Tracey Meharg, Justine Poole

Creative Director: Marylouise Brammer
International Sales Director: Mark Newman
CEO & Publisher: Anne Wilson

ISBN 1 85391 794 X

Printed by Toppan Printing Hong Kong Co. Ltd. PRINTED IN CHINA
First Printed 1999
©Design and photography Murdoch Books® 1999
©Text Le Cordon Bleu 1999

A catalogue record for this book is available from the British Library.

Distributed in the UK by D Services, 6 Euston Street, Freemen's Common, Leicester LE2 7SS Tel 0116-254-7671 Fax 0116-254-4670.
Distributed in Canada by Whitecap (Vancouver) Ltd, 351 Lynn Avenue, North Vancouver, BC V7J 2C4 Tel 604-980-9852 Fax 604-980-8197 or Whitecap (Ontario) Ltd, 47 Coldwater Road, North York, ON M3B 1Y8 Tel 416-444-3442 Fax 416-444-6630
Published and distributed in Australia by Murdoch Books®, GPO Box 1203, Sydney NSW 1045

The Publisher and Le Cordon Bleu wish to thank Villeroy & Boch Australia Pty Ltd. and Waterford Wedgwood Australia Ltd. for their assistance in the photography
Front cover: Seafood paella

IMPORTANT INFORMATION

CONVERSION GUIDE
1 cup = 250 ml (8 fl oz)
1 Australian tablespoon = 20 ml (4 teaspoons)
1 UK tablespoon = 15 ml (3 teaspoons)

NOTE: We have used 20 ml tablespoons. If you are using a 15 ml tablespoon, for most recipes the difference will be negligible. For recipes using baking powder, gelatine, bicarbonate of soda and flour, add an extra teaspoon for each tablespoon specified.

CUP CONVERSIONS—DRY INGREDIENTS
1 cup flour, plain or self-raising = 125 g (4 oz)
1 cup sugar, caster = 250 g (8 oz)
1 cup breadcrumbs, dry = 125 g (4 oz)

IMPORTANT: Those who might be at risk from the effects of salmonella food poisoning (the elderly, pregnant women, young children and those suffering from immune deficiency diseases) should consult their GP with any concerns about eating raw eggs.

64 *seafood*